what
means to me

Bob Carr MP grew up in what is now his electorate of Maroubra, attended the University of New South Wales and worked as a journalist at the ABC and *The Bulletin* before being elected in 1983 to the New South Wales Parliament. In 1988 he was elected unopposed as Leader of the Opposition and in 1995 became the thirteenth Labor Premier of New South Wales. He received the Fulbright Fiftieth Anniversary Distinguished Fellow Award in 2000. His bestselling collection, *Thoughtlines: Reflections of a Public Man*, was published by Penguin Books in 2002.

BOB CARR

what australia means to me

Drawings by Alan Moir

PENGUIN BOOKS

Penguin Books

Published by the Penguin Group
Penguin Books Australia Ltd
250 Camberwell Road, Camberwell, Victoria 3124, Australia
Penguin Books Ltd
80 Strand, London WC2R 0RL, England
Penguin Putnam Inc.
375 Hudson Street, New York, New York 10014, USA
Penguin Books, a division of Pearson Canada
10 Alcorn Avenue, Toronto, Ontario, Canada M4V 3B2
Penguin Books (NZ) Ltd
Cnr Rosedale and Airborne Roads, Albany, Auckland, New Zealand
Penguin Books (South Africa) (Pty) Ltd
24 Sturdee Avenue, Rosebank, Johannesburg 2196, South Africa
Penguin Books India (P) Ltd
11, Community Centre, Panchsheel Park, New Delhi 110 017, India

First published by Penguin Books Australia Ltd 2003

1 3 5 7 9 10 8 6 4 2

Cover design by Louise Leffler, Penguin Design Studio
Text design by Leonie Stott, Penguin Design Studio
Author photography by Earl Carter
Typeset in Minion by Midland Typesetters, Maryborough, Victoria
Printed and bound in Australia by McPherson's Printing Group,
Maryborough, Victoria

National Library of Australia
Cataloguing-in-Publication data:

Carr, Bob, 1947– .
What Australia means to me.

ISBN 0 14 300160 4.

1. Australian essays. I. Moir, Alan, 1947– . II. Title.

A824.4

www.penguin.com.au

To all who suffered in Bali

Foreword

One of the aims of the Australia Day Council of New South Wales is to encourage Australians to reflect on the future, as well as the history, of their country and the character of its people.

We asked Bob Carr, the President of the Council, to set down his ideas about Australian patriotism. His thoughts, expressed in speeches and articles over the years, are brought together for the first time for publication for Australia Day 2003.

Bob Carr is known for his love of history and his contributions to the world of ideas. The views expressed here contain much to stimulate and challenge us, whatever our opinions.

We hope this book will prompt readers to think more about Australia's history and what patriotism might mean in a rapidly changing world.

John Trevillian
Chief Executive Officer
Australia Day Council of New South Wales

In Australia alone is to be found the grotesque, the weird, the strange scribblings of nature learning how to write. Some see no beauty in our trees without shade, our flowers without perfume, our birds who cannot fly, and our beasts who have not yet learnt to walk on all fours. But the dweller in the wilderness acknowledges this fantastic land of monstrosities. He becomes familiar with the beauty of loneliness. Whispered to by the myriad tongues of the wilderness, he learns the language of the barren and the uncouth, and can read the hieroglyphs of the haggard gum-trees, blown into odd shapes, distorted with fierce hot winds, or cramped with cold nights, when the Southern Cross freezes in a cloudless sky of icy blue.

– Marcus Clarke, in his introduction
to Adam Lindsay Gordon's
Sea Spray and Smoke Drift, 1867

Not long ago, in a drawer at home, I came across one of my first books. It was called *The Australia Book*, it was published in the early 1950s and the author was Eve Pownall. On the inside cover under the words 'This book belongs to . . .' I had proudly pencilled 'Robert Carr'. It was the lettering of a six- or seven-year-old staking ownership of his first history book.

The binding is loose now, the paper torn. But I soon found myself looking again, with the curiosity of a boy, at the familiar pages, the simple unpatronising text, the charming old-fashioned drawings of

Aborigines, convicts, bushrangers, diggers. Familiarity came flooding back. This is how it begins:

> The first Australians had been in the land so long
> that no man, not even the oldest, could say how
> they first came here. They were a thin dark
> people and the land gave them all they needed.
>
> For countless years they had lived in the land,
> on the hot inland plains where the sun burned
> the grasses and dried up the billabongs, or in
> the kinder regions where rivers flowed and the
> sea gave them food. There, poised on rocks as
> dark as themselves, they could look over the
> wide blue waters that hid their land from the
> rest of the world . . . The rain filled the rivers
> where they stood . . . The moon watched their
> feastings . . .

After all these years those words are still powerful. Because I knew the banksia scrub and sandstone cliffs between Maroubra and La Perouse where I grew up in the 1950s, it was easy to imagine pre-European Australia. The flavour of my childhood, my sense of nostalgic rediscovery, may have had something to do with it. So it was that more than half a century ago a writer was able to explain – to one Australian child at least – something about the link between the land and indigenous Australians.

'For countless years they had lived in the land . . .' – that knowledge was not something that first came to us with Mabo or the Reconciliation Movement. I think we always understood it, but buried it: as we did in 1901, when our new Constitution refused to count indigenous Australians; or in 1938, when our sesqui-centenary celebrations failed to mention them (and, in the first sign of Aboriginal protest, a small group of Menindee people, objecting to a re-enactment of Arthur Phillip's landing, conceived the idea of a Day of Mourning).

If patriotism springs first from knowledge of our country's history and geography, I have Eve Pownall and her book to thank for getting me started. It awakened my curiosity about Australia's past, its flavours and its stories.

But an understanding of our country takes more than knowledge. It takes imagination. Imagine what the arrival of that First Fleet must have meant to the first Australians – the first sight of those strange vessels on that calm, sultry morning. Picture seeing them, as the Eora people did, through the fringe of eucalypt and acacia that extended to the water's edge: the uniforms of Phillip and his men, the ghostly faces, the babble of Irish and Cockney accents.

Were the Eora aware that morning that their way of life was threatened? And what of the women on the beach at La Perouse, eighteen years earlier, shouting to Cook and his men to go away? Did they know then that this was the beginning of the end of life as they knew it, that the country that was theirs was lost, about to change forever? I suspect that they did, at least in part.

What is it that we really love about Australia? What is it that we celebrate on Australia Day? What is it – remembering the dark things in our past – that gives us the *right* to celebrate? What does patriotism mean for us? Is there, perhaps, a special kind of patriotism for Australians?

I think there is. And in this essay I will try to explain it.

A funny, friendly, benign country

Ten years ago, I said in a speech that there were three elements in an Australian patriotism. The first was our response to the land itself, unique and beautiful. The second was the people. I said we were a 'motley' people, and I meant that in the most generous way, meaning an immigrant people, from diverse sources – indeed, almost every country in the world. There are not many societies – the USA and Canada, perhaps Israel – with such diversity. In a quarter of the homes in New South Wales lives someone who was born overseas.

The third element, I said, was the unusual society that resulted from the interaction of that land and that people: a working democracy where the rule of law prevails, where the fairness of policies is the essence of the political debate. In my speech I called it a funny, friendly, benign country.

A happy country, too. During the Olympics, among the crowds in Martin Place and East Circular Quay, in the throngs of country people and visitors from interstate, I often thought as I mingled with them: 'This has to be the *happiest* place in the world, the happiest people – at the best time in our history!' It was their good humour that persuaded me there is no country happier than this – a country that comes to a halt for a horse race, whose most successful comedian is a madcap female impersonator. It's a country that has the weirdest animals, none of them predators. A country where the birds laugh at us. A funny country, in the nicest way.

Perhaps I'd add now: an unpretentious country. For what I'd like to see is a patriotism without pomposity, never solemn or grandiose, and never saccharine. It would be a patriotism based on reality rather than symbols or theories. It would come from a recognition of things as they are and as they were, not a vision of what dreamers or zealots would like us to be. Not a blind, uncritical, my-country-right-or-wrong patriotism. It would acknowledge the dark side of our beginnings, our failings as well as our achievements, both the good side and the bad side, because Australian history has many stories. And this is a helpful notion: we don't have to choose a black-armband view or a celebratory white-settler view. History doesn't have to be a choice. History is different stories. And they can live side by side, merge and overlap, jostle and elbow one another.

Clearing away old myths

But first we have to clear away some myths, some old habits of mind.

The first is the myth that we are a young country. It's an idea enshrined in our national anthem: 'for we are young and free'. We are 'young' only in terms of European perceptions. Our indigenous people are the oldest surviving human culture. Geologically, we are the oldest continent on earth. In political terms, we are among the most mature societies in the world. Not many have had continuous parliamentary systems since the mid-nineteenth century.

And that's how we should think of ourselves: grown-up and confident. The idea of Australia as a young country suggests there's a mother country

.. GIRT-BY- SEA....

willing to take care of us. We shook off that particular delusion in 1942 when Britain had too much else on its hands. Or in 1962 when she opted to enter the European Common Market. I still remember the shock in my classroom at Matraville High when we discussed it. 'Could this mean the end of the Commonwealth?' a girl asked the teacher in shaken tones. 'It could mean that,' came the sober reply. Unimaginable – Australia not part of the *British* Commonwealth, all those pink spaces on the world map!

Remember that many countries in Europe today did not exist when Australia became a nation in 1901. Even fourteen years ago there were two Germanys, no independent Baltic states, no separate Russia, no independent Central Asian republics. In terms of political independence, we are older than all of them. As a political entity we are older than most of the countries of Africa, older than Indonesia, older than Pakistan.

Another myth is the idea that we're a distant country, remote from the world, far from the great centres of power and ideas. Again this is a European view. After the Bali bombing, no one believes it. We are not remote from Jakarta or Singapore or Kuala Lumpur. We are scarcely more remote from Afghanistan than New York or Washington are. Indonesia, the world's largest Islamic state, is our neighbour. The idea that Australia is a distant country encourages insularity and complacency. Australia is simply another part of the world.

Then there's the myth that we are underpopulated. I'll come back to this later. It took hold during the gold rushes, when Australians entertained the idea that we could be a continental power like the USA and could fill our wide, open spaces just as the Americans did. But we ran into problems: thin soil, dry rivers, low rainfall, sparse vegetation. In the 1920s, when Griffith Taylor, a geographer at the University of Sydney, suggested an optimum population of only twenty million – he was ridiculed for his conservatism and run out of town. Now we know more about our country's limitations.

Another myth: the idea that we're good at sport and not much else. The best news I read last year wasn't in the sports pages. It was the announcement that the hole in the ozone layer, the result mainly of fluorocarbon emissions, is expected to close by 2050. I felt pride when our CSIRO scientists announced that news. Of course, it isn't all our doing, but it was a good reminder of our scientific strength. It also showed that international environmental protocols can work when enough countries get behind them. It was a reminder that we are part of the planet. So let us, even now, get behind Kyoto.

REMEMBER . . WE ARE FURTHER FROM THEM THAN THEY ARE FROM US . .
SE ASIA

Talking up Australia as a 'sporting nation' only reinforces a stereotype – and you can always lose a sporting medal. I take the same pride as anyone in our sporting achievements. After all, we had a national cricket team – back in the 1860s – well before we had a national parliament. Visit the Bradman Museum in Bowral and see how one sport flavoured our national life. Sporting successes send an up-beat, happy-warrior image of Australia to the world (and any attention a middle or regional power like Australia can get is a good thing). But if we hadn't won a single medal at the Sydney Olympics, those Games would still have been a triumph for us – a triumph of planning, of organisation, of a cooperative society getting things done. It's one reason New South Wales and Victoria are leading the push to host the soccer World Cup in Australia in 2014.

That news about the ozone layer set me thinking about other achievements – all the ways we have improved our lives in recent years. Half as many of us are dying of heart disease as twenty years ago. Smoking, with its huge cost in ruined lives, is no longer the smart thing to do. Australia has one of the best records of beating the public health challenge of HIV/AIDS. Look at our harbours and beaches: cleaner, healthier. Sydney Harbour cleaner now than ever in a hundred years. I can swim at Maroubra or

Clovelly without fearing sewage grease blown in by a southerly. We're cutting the road toll, with fatalities four times lower today than they were in 1967. Never have Australians been more aware of the fragile beauty of the natural world, the importance of historic buildings, our wildlife, the techniques of bush regeneration. Thirty-five years ago there was hardly a place for women in parliament, on the bench, in business or in the boardroom. All that has changed.

And in a quiet way we're winning on alcoholism, on literacy, on aged people's care, on safety in the workplace. There's hope on drugs. We're more alert to the needs of the disabled: every new building, bus and railway station in New South Wales is now wheelchair-accessible. We've stopped people rorting the system with outrageous public-liability claims, reversing a trend towards a culture of litigation. A visitor from California was almost dumbstruck at how we had turned that tendency around.

Something like that shows our arteries haven't hardened, we can be flexible, move fast. We saw it in the transformation of the Australian economy after 1983. We were highly protected, sluggish and inward-looking until the burst of reformist energy released by the first decisions of the Hawke–Keating Government to float the currency. Without that impetus Australia could not have enjoyed the productivity growth and economic performance of the 1990s. It is hard to be proud of a country that gets economic decisions consistently wrong, easier to relate to a national performance that has us competing with the best. Without the streamlined economic perform- ance we enjoyed in the last decade, it would be hard to think confidently about Australia's future.

In any case, modernity becomes us. Modern air terminals, transport systems, the latest generation of city buildings and street furniture and public works: 'You've got a *snappy* place here,' a Walt Disney execu- tive told me. I took to that description, a 'snappy' place. The pride of Australians in the look of Sydney during the Olympics was irrepressible. That look reflected the emergence of a high-productivity, world-competitive economy. Creaking, clapped-out economies give little reason for pride. The latest generation of Australians produced a burst of modernisation.

These, I stress, have all been *national* achieve- ments. They show a capacity to adapt and think smartly. They should form a part of how we see ourselves. They should feed a quiet, unassertive pride, a self-esteem at the core of a new Australian patriotism.

MY TIME MACHINE

If you had a time machine, what episodes in Australian history would you visit?

Here are my choices.

Somewhere in the early Dreamtime, to experience an Australia of endless coastal forests, teeming with wildlife, with the ancestors of today's Aborigines executing their earliest paintings and carvings or stalking kangaroos over vast distances, inventing their mythologies and stories.

Sydney Cove in 1788, to see the first European settlers come ashore in their boats, venturing their first steps on a weird new land, a world away from the filthy Georgian London of Boswell and Hogarth. A little later, to see them launch Australia's first party – a drunken celebration of sailors and convicts under the eucalypts, amid the rocks, until a southerly buster sent them scattering for cover. Who among them brought their copy of Shakespeare or Dr Johnson's dictionary?

Unity Hall, Balmain, Sydney, in 1891, to witness the first branch meeting of what would become the Australian Labor Party. Manual workers meeting to launch (audaciously) their own political party, to better protect their families. In so doing, they were extending Australian democracy.

Sydney in January 1901, to see the birth of Australian Federation – not the official ceremony in Centennial Park, all plumed hats and heavy serge suits, but earlier, in the streets, as crowds cheered the parade of floats and bands in happy celebration of the launch of a new nation. Among the faces: visitors from the bush, boys who would become Anzacs.

I was going to nominate Martin Place in Sydney in 1945, to see the celebrations of VE Day (in May) and VJ Day (in August) at the end of World War II. But now, I think, another date: **13 October 1945, at the dockside at Circular Quay**, for the arrival of the British aircraft carrier HMS *Formidable*, bringing home one of the largest groups of Australian prisoners of war, including many from the notorious Changi camp in Singapore. I want to see them as their feet again touch Australia's blessed soil and their families rush forward.

The Tally Room in Canberra in 1951, to see the referendum results flowing in to defeat Robert Menzies' plan to ban the Communist Party. A seminal moment: at the height of the Cold War we would not ban a political organisation, even one pledged to the overthrow of our government. We would stay democratic.

The Olympics Opening Ceremony on 15 September 2000, to watch again that incomparable pageant, an encapsulation of our history and ethos, and for me one of the great works of art produced by Australians.

The dark side

But there's a dark side, too. The men and women who arrived with Arthur Phillip on those eleven ships of the First Fleet were entering a country they had never seen or imagined, with its shy, nocturnal creatures, its fragile soil. Not only had the soil never been trodden by Europeans, it had scarcely been trodden at all. It was virgin soil. Eric Rolls, a poet as well as a naturalist and historian, has put it well:

> The surface was so loose that you could rake it through the fingers. No wheel had marked it, no leather heel, no cloven foot – every mammal, humans included, had walked on padded feet. Our big animals did not make trails. Hopping kangaroos usually move in scattered company, not in damaging single file like sheep and cattle . . . No other land had been treated so gently.

In crushing that untrodden soil we crushed the lives of the people it nurtured. The European settlers not only took the land of the original Australians, they degraded it. We are still paying the cost of that damage in erosion, dry-land salinity, acid sulfate soils, occasional dust storms in the cities.

For those first settlers, the landscape had to be

confronted and subdued, like the indigenous people. Even the English language – that glorious inheritance (one of our luckiest) from the Old World – was inadequate to describe what they saw. Words such as 'dust', 'drought', 'flood' and 'plain' are all English words, but they are not words that belong to English experience, to the English landscape. As the poet Geoffrey Lehmann has written, 'drought was for the Anglo-Saxon more of a spiritual state, but here it was an actual physical thing which you experienced. Dust was something you feared your body would become. Here it was something which could choke the sky for days on end.'

Australian humour

If our landscape at first seemed mythological to the Europeans, what ultimately made it real for them? I think it was the suffering of the pioneers. All the hardship and privation they experienced was expressed in the bush ballads of the nineteenth century – 'a mixture,' as Lehmann put it, 'of humour and pain with a dash of apocalypse'. Humour is the quality I was talking about when I spoke of a funny, friendly country. It's one of the keys to an Australian patriotism.

I like the way we look with amusement on much that others take seriously: pomposity in high places, empty ceremony, excessive flag-waving, elaborate class distinction. Fascism could not have taken off here. The generation of my mother and father would have scoffed at a grimacing Mussolini or Blackshirt uniforms.

It's no coincidence that we've produced so many humorists: Steele Rudd, Roy Rene, George Wallace, Ross Campbell, Dawn Lake, Lennie Lower, Barry Humphries. We've even had funny politicians: George Reid, Fred Daly, Les Haylen, Barry Cohen, Jim Killen. There's something admirable about a country that boasts of its prowess in cartooning, where comic-strip characters created in the pain of the Depression, or earlier, survive in folklore and memory. Humour was the first protection of the early settlers against disaster, the terrors of a continent disturbed. And reading the bush poets and balladeers you'll find a trace of humour in even their harshest thoughts.

> It was the middle of the drought; the ground was
>   hot and bare,
> You might search the grass with a microscope,
>   but nary grass was there;
> The hay was done, the cornstalks gone, the trees
>   were dying fast,
> The sun o'erhead was a curse in red and the
>   wind was a furnace blast;

The waterholes were sunbaked mud, the drays
   stood thick as bees
Around the well, a mile away, amid the
   ringbarked trees.

Has there been a more pitiless description of drought than these lines by George Essex Evans? They were written during Australia's longest drought, the one that scorched an entire continent more than a century ago, from 1895 to 1903, inspiring a famous joke by Bill Wannan, one of our great storytellers, that the drought wouldn't be over until bush folk could have water in their tea. Our farmers, our bush people, still take comfort in humour. In all the days and hours I've spent with them in recent months, I've seen that humour sustain them.

The journals of the First Fleet, among all their dry observations about winds and weather and daily provisions, include one funny detail. They reveal that on 2 January 1788 convicts aboard the *Scarborough* staged 'a dramatic entertainment'. Think of it. Their ship many miles off the coast of South Australia, battling the Roaring Forties. Imagine how the sea might have been that night, how distant and intimidating the chill, starlit sky. But as the little ship ploughed forward on its creaking path, the people aboard staged an entertainment to cheer themselves.

We have no record of what it was. David Malouf, in his magnificent series of Boyer Lectures in 1998, saw it as a response to the misery of cramped conditions and the terrors awaiting the convicts on their fatal shore. Can we see in that brief interlude of theatrical make-believe the first expression of the Australian taste for fun and games – the quality Malouf defined, in the title of his lectures, as 'a spirit of play' – the quest for happiness, the spirit cruelly assaulted in Bali? For Malouf, what saved Australia during its harshest trials was 'neighbourliness, the saving grace of lightness and good humour, the choice of moderation over the temptation to any form of extreme' (again, think of our response to the Depression – no fascists here). I believe it is this lightness of spirit, this humour – linking so many other strands in our national temperament, from a love of gambling to the love of sport itself – that sustains us now, as we confront the evils of terrorism and the scourges of drought and fire.

In all sorts of ways we've defined new forms of Australian humour. We've brought a fresh kind of jokiness to Australian films. 'I love the *naïvete* of your movies,' an American once told me. Even the list of Australian inventions reads like a catalogue of quirkiness: the cardboard wine cask, the Esky, the Hills hoist, the stump-jump plough. (The early bushmen praised the 'emu-egg omelette' and 'paddymelon stew'.)

There's something spirited and inventive, too, in our use of language. In his dictionary of Australian colloquialisms, G. A. Wilkes noted that Australians had given a new life to many dialect words neglected by the English ('dinkum' was one), while appropriating other words – 'billabong', 'boomerang', 'corroboree' – from Aboriginal languages. (The land wasn't the only thing we stole from the first Australians.)

On the last night of the Sydney Olympic Games, as we left the Closing Ceremony, I spotted Henry Kissinger. I wondered how he took to the quirky humour, the Shark playing golf and the rest. Perhaps apologetically I found myself saying, 'You know, we're a funny country, Henry.' He said, seriously, 'This is the only other country in the world I'd consider living in.'

Bill Bryson, the American writer, in his survey of the English language, *Mother Tongue*, noted our gift for colourful slang. I doubt if it matters that few of us use our quaint old slang terms today. It is unlikely that any young Australian says 'bonzer' or 'extra grouse' any more. But they stand as reminders of a nonchalant, high-spirited, irreverent and sometimes rebellious temperament that we like to call

our own. It's part of what Ken Burns called, in his definition of history, our 'emotional archaeology'.

There is a link between this sense of humour – being a funny country – and having a deeply ingrained respect for fair play. Not taking yourself too seriously means that you think a little more seriously about others. D. H. Lawrence, who saw Australia as the first genuine democracy, noted that humour and a sense of fairness went together. Richard Somers, who stands for Lawrence in his novel *Kangaroo*, recalls after a visit to Australia: 'There was really no class distinction. There was a difference of money and of "smartness". But nobody felt *better* than anyone else, or higher; only *better-off*.' When Lawrence was writing in 1922 many men were better off, but there were none of today's gross disparities of personal income. Australians of the 1920s would be horrified to see Australian CEOs earning fifty times or more the average worker's pay. But, in essence, he was right. Lawrence, by the way, wasn't starry-eyed about Australia, but he was in no doubt about our decency, our fair play, our sense of humour.

Our heroes

In my search for a valid Australian patriotism I want to look again at our heroes. Other nations find it difficult to acknowledge faults in their heroes. Thomas Jefferson was one of the heroes of the American Revolution, a political thinker of genius. But he was also a slave-owner. All his nation building was done on the back of slave labour.

Acknowledging the 'Jeffersons' in our own history – the flawed heroes – is an essential part of getting our patriotism in perspective. Recall some of the founders and shapers of our institutions: W. M. Hughes, who called himself an Australian patriot and devoted most of his energies to campaigns to conscript Australians for the battle-fields of Europe; Henry Parkes, renowned as the Father of Federation, a sectarian bigot who practised a poisonous brand of anti-Catholic, anti-Irish politics; John Macarthur, founder of the wool industry, an intriguer and wrecker who died with his mind destroyed; Bob Menzies, one of our great prime ministers, who called himself 'British to the boot-heels' and launched an assault on Australian civil liberties in 1951 that has few parallels among Westminster democracies; Owen Dixon, internationally renowned as Chief Justice of the High Court, who, in Geoffrey Robertson's words, 'discouraged the Privy

Council developing as a true Commonwealth Court because he was physically revolted by the prospect of sitting alongside a black judge'; or Bert Evatt, that erratic idealist, one of the first presidents of the UN General Assembly and one of the great wreckers of his party, the ALP.

Often it would seem that failure, compromise and disgrace have been the distinguishing qualities of our leaders. Gough Whitlam wrote in 1971 about E. G. Theodore, Treasurer during the Depression:

> There is a deep poignancy in the fate of a
> remarkably long list of our chief figures from
> the very beginning: Phillip embittered and
> exhausted; Bligh disgraced; Macquarie
> despised here and discredited at home;
> Macarthur mad; Wentworth rejecting the
> meaning of his own achievements; Parkes
> bankrupt; Deakin out-living his superb
> faculties in a long twilight of senility; Fisher
> forgotten; Bruce living in self-chosen exile;
> Scullin heartbroken; Lyons dying in the midst
> of relentless intrigue against him; Curtin
> driven to desperation and to the point
> of resignation by some of his own colleagues
> at the worst period in the war. Theodore's
> particular tragedy was that of a supremely

able man suddenly struck powerless at the
very time when his power and his ability
were at their peak and most needed.

He might have added today: Holt drowned with his
government in disarray; Gorton deposed; McMahon
ridiculed and defeated; Whitlam himself dismissed
by the Governor-General he appointed; Hawke,
Labor's greatest vote-winner, rejected by his own
party; Keating, one of our true visionaries, humili-
ated by the voters.

If I had to suggest some new Australian heroes,
I would first ask that we re-evaluate our old ones.
I'd appeal for a moratorium on excessive adulation
of Sir Donald Bradman. Magnificent cricketer
though he was, I am told even the Don himself
was embarrassed by the fawning attention he
received from the media. I have never understood
the cult of Ned Kelly: a killer, an armed robber,
a home invader, despite the efforts of Sidney Nolan,
Peter Carey, Douglas Stewart, Robert Drewe and
more than one filmmaker to mythologise him in
art and literature.

I'd get Peter Lalor and the Eureka Stockade into
perspective. There was a time when communists and
their sympathisers claimed Eureka as a proletarian
uprising, the beginnings of Australian democracy.

Of course it wasn't. As Geoffrey Blainey saw it, the rebellion paved the way for capitalism on the gold-fields. An insurrection by a handful of miners and landholders over an increase in licence charges was put down by a force of mounted troops. Five soldiers and thirty miners died that day. Others may disagree, but it is difficult not to conclude that their deaths meant nothing and achieved nothing.

In fact our early heroes weren't revolutionaries or martyrs or freedom fighters. Democracy, then nation-hood, came easily. Our knowledge of war has been gained largely on other people's soil. Australia as a nation-state was voted into existence by its future citizens. We've built a modern nation from scratch.

I discovered some of my heroes in 1999 when I visited an Australian sacred site, the Australian War Memorial in Canberra. I wrote then: 'It is good to know terrible things, although they are hard to bear.' Eve Pownall had taught me some of those terrible things in my child's history book, but they meant little to me. War has scant meaning for those fortu-nate children who have never experienced it.

Among my heroes is William Matthew Keating, thirty-six years old when he died on a death march in North Borneo during the Japanese occupation in World War II. A total of 1787 Australians died on that march – exhausted, beaten, tortured, starved. You can see their faces – the size of passport photos – on the walls of the memorial, taken when they signed up. William Matthew Keating's nephew became Prime Minister of Australia.

One of the survivors of the march was Keith Botterill of Lithgow. He tells in a video interview how one of his mates was tied to a stake for ten days and kicked by Japanese guards. Elsewhere is the photo of Sergeant Len Siffleet of Gunnedah, kneeling to be beheaded by a Japanese sword. The famous image of his last moment on earth was found on the body of a Japanese officer.

I learned other things in that war museum that day: that 5000 Australians died in the skies over Europe in World War II – over Berlin, Frankfurt, Bremen, or busting the Mohne and Eder dams. I learned that more Australians died in World War I – 61 720 – than Americans in Vietnam. It was the same war – the 'Great War' – that produced Gallipoli, that defining moment in the Australian story when men scaled that flinty hillside 'in a raked, boot-scrambling roar' – Les Murray's words – 'to the heights of thyme and rosemary'. It was the war that produced another of my heroes, John Monash, the greatest of Australian soldiers. Anthony Eden called him 'the best soldier of the war'. Monash was great because he declined to throw waves of troops at the German trenches. He built a strategy around minimising losses, but won victories that helped bring that war to an end.

I learned that 240 Australians died in the Darwin air raid of 1942. That raid was our Pearl Harbor (just as Bali was our September 11). In one gallery of the museum you learn of the Japanese midget submarine that surfaced in Sydney Harbour one night in May 1942 and sank a ferry. In 1942 people were walking *away* from harbourside real estate, heading for the North Shore or the Blue Mountains. Far from being a source of delight, the harbour was a source of danger – a link with a hostile world, as it must have seemed to the Eora people for a time.

Other wars had been fought on Australian soil, though no one ever declared them. They have, as yet, no honour rolls or memorials. They were the wars between indigenous inhabitants and early settlers and police. We have little idea how many indigenous people were slaughtered. We know something of isolated atrocities, such as the massacre in 1838 at Myall Creek of twenty-eight Aboriginal men, women and children, for which the perpetrators were hanged. For the writer Tony Stephens, Australian innocence might have died when the Aborigines were wiped out in Tasmania, or when a Constable Murray, who had fought at Gallipoli, with his vigilante party shot dead up to seventy Aborigines around Coniston, in the

MY AUSTRALIAN HEROES

Most people would nominate their **individual heroes**: Arthur Phillip, Edmund Barton, Henry Parkes, Matthew Flinders, Howard Florey, Caroline Chisholm, John Monash, John Curtin, Francis Greenway, Albert Namatjira, Douglas Mawson, Henry Lawson, Fred Hollows, Eddie Mabo, Don Bradman, Jessie Street, Faith Bandler, Ben Chifley, Gough Whitlam.

But I take a different approach – to elevate our anonymous and uncounted heroes.

The Aborigines who first crossed the Blue Mountains.

The convict builders celebrated by Mary Gilmore in her poem 'Old Botany Bay':

I split the rock;
I felled the tree:
The nation was –
Because of me!

The multicultural work force that built the Snowy Mountains Scheme and the Sydney Opera House, and the monocultural one that built the Sydney Harbour Bridge between 1923 and 1932.

All the artists and dancers who gave us the Olympic Opening Ceremony, a spectacular celebration of our working people – such as those who gave us an iron and steel industry after 1917.

Our **shearers**, commemorated in Tom Roberts's *Shearing the Rams*, one of the few images of labour in any art of the Impressionist era.

The **nurses** who served in many wars.

Those 10 000 women, dressed in black, who marched from the Sydney Domain to Woolloomooloo in 1918 to honour Australia's dead in World War I.

The troops who enlisted to fight World War II before the end of 1939, known thereafter as **the 39ers**.

The soldiers on the Kokoda Track who turned back the Japanese advance in New Guinea in 1942 and 1943, stopping the Japanese within 40 kilometres of Port Moresby, inflicting a crucial defeat and helping turn the tide of war at a cost of 6000 Australian lives. And those who fought at **Milne Bay**.

In fact, that generation: born in World War I, who entered the work force in the Depression (often not able to find a job), who enlisted for World War II, and then were part of that relatively austere life of reconstruction after 1945. **My parents' generation**, a whole generation of heroes.

Northern Territory, in 1928. A story like that should freeze us in our tracks. The historian Henry Reynolds has suggested that accounts of these frontier wars be included with the other exhibits at the Australian War Memorial. There would have been heroes in those wars, too, if only we knew their names.

My heroes include our scientists, amongst the most neglected of our nation builders and intellectual pathfinders. Peter Doherty grew up in Brisbane and won the Nobel Prize for Medicine in 1996 (together with his Swiss colleague Rolf Zinkernagel) for research that transformed our understanding of the human immune system. If the world were to experience another flu epidemic like the one that killed fifty million people between 1918 and 1922, Doherty's research could save millions of lives.

Here's a date to remember: 27 October 1977. It was the day Ali Maow Maalin, a cook at a hospital in Somalia, contracted smallpox. Maalin was the last person in the world to catch smallpox. The defeat of smallpox was a scientific triumph – which makes its threatened use by terrorists more appalling. Perhaps we'll see a day when Australian scientists identify the last victims of Alzheimer's or leukaemia, multiple sclerosis, schizophrenia or HIV/AIDS.

Will another Peter Doherty break the news that motor neurone disease is a thing of the past? We have some of the best medical research teams in the world. Australians have won more Nobel prizes in science and medicine, in proportion to our numbers, than any other people. Consider the pantheon to which Peter Doherty belongs: Howard Florey, a pioneer in the use of antibiotics, whose work may have saved more lives than Lister or Pasteur (Florey shared the Nobel Prize for Medicine in 1945); John Eccles (Nobel Prize winner for Medicine in 1963 for his work in detecting electrical impulses in the brain); Macfarlane Burnet (Nobel Prize winner for Medicine in 1960 for his work in immunobiology); John Cornforth (Nobel Prize winner for Chemistry in 1975); Mark Oliphant, who worked on the first atomic bomb in Los Alamos and became a peace advocate (as well as a governor of South Australia); Ian Clunies Ross, head of the CSIRO when Australian scientists were successfully tackling the rabbit plague.

My heroes include Helena Mills, daughter of James Patrick Garvan, Treasurer of New South Wales for three months in 1889 and founder of the MLC Insurance Company, who gave her estate to establish the Garvan Institute of Medical Research as a memorial to her father. Today it is a leader in biotechnology research.

My heroes include bushfire fighters, the armies of volunteer workers who made the Sydney Olympics

the best in the world, our servicemen and women
in Afghanistan and East Timor and the Persian
Gulf, police who risk their lives in the line of duty,
nurses, bushwalking conservationists, parents, charity
workers, teachers, carers, artists, industrialists. The
quiet heroes of Bali. Countless people whose names
we don't know and many whose names we do.

They include Tan Le, who with her mother and
sister escaped from Vietnam in 1976. They set out for
Australia in a little boat when Tan Le was four. After
five days and nights on the open sea, they were
rescued by a British tanker. In 1998 Tan Le graduated
with honours in Commerce and Law from Monash
University. She has organised arts events in Melbourne. Her mother has served as Mayor of Mari-
byrnong in Melbourne's inner west. In 1998 Tan Le
was named Young Australian of the Year.

They include Essington Lewis, head of BHP for
thirty years from 1921 to 1951, when he made Australia a world leader in iron and steel production, show-
ing how a predominantly rural economy of farming
and grazing could diversify into heavy industry, construction and engineering.

They include Jørn Utzon, architect of the Sydney
Opera House, the stoic, sunny, open-hearted Dane
who gave Australia the most beautiful building in the
world, the symbol of our nation. When he was driven

home in humiliation, he refused to succumb to bitterness or despair, and now is working for us again on the building he loved, and has never seen.

They include Shirley Perry Smith: welfare worker; prison visitor; friend of the homeless and dispossessed; born on the Erambie Mission, near Cowra, of Wiradjuri descent; mother and carer to more than sixty children in need; known and honoured as 'Mum Shirl' for her work for Aborigines.

They include Faith Bandler, daughter of a Kanak slave, a bold voice in the struggle for Aboriginal rights in the 1960s, especially in the crucial referendum of 1967; and Jessie Street, a valiant fighter for human rights conventions after World War II (and whose son, husband and father-in-law were all notable chief justices of New South Wales); the pioneer reformer Caroline Chisholm and those other brave fighters for women, the poet Mary Gilmore and Louisa Lawson (mother of Henry) who ran a feminist newspaper for seventeen years and never yielded to hostility or scorn.

The British heritage

Let's return to that first sultry morning, to those first heroes, the founders of modern Australia. Whatever we may think of the system they served, Cook and Phillip were among the noblest of people, and we can appropriate them as Australians – at least, I want to. European maritime exploration until Cook's day had been for military and imperialistic purposes. Cook's three voyages in the late eighteenth century were devoted to the study of natural science and astronomy. We were a country born in the spirit of scientific inquiry.

Contemporaries of Cook spoke of his humanity, his forbearance, his kindness to his men. Phillip was in some ways an even more admirable figure – generous, civilised, courageous. Well schooled in the humanities, he spoke four languages – English, German, French, Portuguese. His father, a German Jew, came from Frankfurt.

Today we might call Phillip the first representative of multicultural Australia. He led his fleet on one of the longest journeys ever made. It was an astonishing achievement. His ships left England in May 1787 crowded with nearly a thousand people, among them more than seven hundred convicts. They set records – in the number of vessels, the number of passengers, the distance travelled. Never before had so many travelled so far, and with so few fatalities. Those voyages were the moon landings of the eighteenth century: humanity venturing into the unknown, into regions unseen and barely imagined by the people of the Old World.

But Phillip brought something else. He was the first to articulate a political philosophy, a founding principle, for the society he established at Port Jackson. Consider this. He had seen something of slavery in Brazil. He had sympathised with the abolitionist cause at home. The laws of New South Wales, he wrote in 1787, would be those of Britain, but there was one law above all he wished to enact from the moment his forces arrived: 'There can be no slavery in a free land, and consequently no slaves.'

Beautiful words, worthy of Abraham Lincoln. But for Phillip no mere rhetoric. Britain had learned from the experience of her American colonies. Some of those colonies had been built by slave labour; the Australian colonies would be built by convicts. And for convicts who had served their time there was freedom. Moreover, a convict's children were *born* free. As Malouf put it: 'If the convict stain remained hard to forget and the brutalities, for some, even harder to forgive, it has not been carried down from generation to generation like the stain of slavery.'

Along with the chains and cruelties, those eleven vessels brought the rudiments of a civilisation: ideas of political rights, of checks on authority, the English genius for tolerance and compromise, intellectual liberalism out of the tradition of the 'Glorious Revolution' of 1688 ('*Very* important, *very* important –

1688,' Margaret Thatcher told me after I invoked its anniversary during her Bicentennial visit here in 1988.) They brought freedom of expression – what the US Justice Oliver Wendell Holmes called 'free trade in the marketplace of ideas' – a large part of what an Australian patriot should celebrate. And it's perfectly consistent, of course, with the idea of a republic – whenever and however it may come.

Finding the words

How much of our patriotism can be expressed in words? I was relieved when voters threw out a preamble for the Constitution in the 1999 referendum. It was full of lumbering bureaucratic phrases ('supportive of achievement', 'mindful of our responsibilities'). The words of our anthem also leave something to be desired, but the old version was worse: 'Australia's *sons*, let us rejoice.'

There are times, however, when we get the words right. More than a hundred thousand people every year earn the right to speak the Oath of Allegiance at their naturalisation ceremony. There's nothing flowery or poetic about those words, but their force and clarity never fail to stir me:

> I pledge my loyalty to Australia and its people
> Whose democratic beliefs I share,

Whose rights and liberties I respect,
Whose laws I will uphold and obey.

Look at those words to see how right they are. Beliefs are something we 'share', they are not to be imposed or blindly accepted. Rights and liberties are something we 'respect'.

We pledge loyalty 'to Australia and its people'. Loyalty is something to be given to our families, to our neighbours, to the Australian people – rather than to abstractions or institutions such as governments, constitutions or heads of state. This is a remarkably enlightened idea. It implies a duty of caring. It may be uniquely Australian. Perhaps it's another way of expressing mateship.

When I speak of a duty of caring, I think of all the ways Australians have shown themselves to be out in front when it comes to caring for our fellows, respecting rights and liberties, building a fair society. Our Labor Party is older than Britain's. We were the first country to elect Labor members of parliament. We were the first country, after New Zealand, to give women the vote. We were among the first to legislate for a basic wage and construct a viable system of arbitration backed by the courts. One of the first with an old-age pension.

We are a country that debates fairness more than

other societies do. It's part of our make-up. Fairness is the first test of everything governments do – and neither side of politics can avoid it. Which tax regime is fairest? Which wages policy? What priorities in social welfare? The idea of the fair go is second nature to Australians – part of what an Australian patriotism encompasses. More than once it has allowed unpopular or threatened governments to be re-elected for a second term: Menzies in 1951, Whitlam in 1974. Donald Horne has given a wider meaning to fairness than just helping the underdog. He saw fairness as the basis of our confidence in the electoral system, in the right to hold opinions and have them heard, in our treatment of minorities. For Horne, fairness is also the basis of our belief in the rule of law. He dubbed it 'a fair go in the courts'.

So an Australian patriotism that values fairness also values the rule of law. It's another idea reflected in the words of the oath: 'Whose laws I will uphold and obey.' We're a working democracy under the rule of law. And what makes us unique – different from other democracies under the rule of law – is that Australians have known nothing else. Throughout most of our history as a modern nation, we have lived under the rule of law in a democratic system.

Somehow our genius has been found in avoiding rallying cries, slogans and bellicose anthems. Our

ESSENTIAL BOOKS ABOUT AUSTRALIA

John Cobley's *Sydney Cove* gives day-by-day extracts from the journals of the First Fleeters from 1788 to 1792.

The first chapter of **Robert Hughes's** *The Fatal Shore* **(1987)** gives a magic description of the world before white settlement, of Sydney Harbour as it was before the first Australia Day.

C. E. W. Bean's *Official History of Australia in the War of 1914–1918* **(1921–42)**, a masterpiece of reporting, military analysis and humane observation of Australians at war.

Manning Clark's *A History of Australia*, **volumes 1–6 (1962–87)**. No, don't read it all. It's not one of those books. Pick a period about which *you* are curious – perhaps the gold rushes or World War I – and devour that slab. Or listen to the taped version read by John Bell. The books have huge flaws but great insights – such as those into the religious mainsprings of the eighteenth-century settlers and the class tensions running through Australian society.

Geoffrey Blainey's *The Tyranny of Distance* **(1966)**, his seminal analysis of Australia's place in the world, as well as two other books by this fine historian: ***The Rush that Never Ended: A History of Australian Mining*** (1963) and his account of indigenous Australia, ***Triumph of the Nomads*** (1975).

Add to this **Henry Reynolds's** more recent, more challenging books on Aboriginal Australia, including his early work ***The Other Side of the Frontier*** (1981).

D. H. Lawrence's novel *Kangaroo* (1923), full of insights into the character of Australia in the 1920s, an affectionate portrait by one of the twentieth century's greatest novelists.

Donald Horne's *The Lucky Country* (1964), a witty and perceptive study of the national ethos, updated ('revisited') in 1984, and still relevant today.

Miles Franklin's *My Brilliant Career* (1901), a cheeky assertion, with its mocking title, that women in Australia wanted to push forward out of constraints and discrimination, to be heard and make a difference.

Gavin Souter's *Lion and Kangaroo* (1976), a wonderful account of Australia's nation-building years between Federation and World War I – that glad confident morning when we were forging a distinct identity.

most famous song – funny and friendly – is about a swagman and a billabong. It's one reason I've never been drawn to a bill of rights – a codification of the privileges and assumptions Australians accept as their birthright. The grand words of a bill of rights can mean nothing. Stalin's 1936 Constitution was full of them. It's why I'm comfortable with an Australian Constitution that is silent on many questions of democratic principle, on rights, fairness, fair play, egalitarianism – the values we most care about. The more you define those rights, the more you can limit their meaning. The more you discuss them, the more they elude you. Leave them uncodified, living in our character. The ethos of an institution is always more important than its rule-book, anyway. An important point, that, about politics and government!

As Donald Horne observed: 'It's one of the oddities of Australia that, although most liberal democratic societies define themselves partly or mainly by their political institutions and principles, we scarcely ever talk about ours in any way that is specific.' I find that the countries that go on about democracy are usually the ones that have less of it – just as the countries with the gaudiest stamps and flashiest banknotes are often among the poorest.

Knowing our history

But without powerful patriotic slogans and rallying cries there is something missing from Australian patriotism, even if it is something nebulous and hard to define. The question is: What do we put in its place?

One thing we can put in its place is a better knowledge of our history.

Here's another date to remember. In December 1855 a sailing ship reached Sydney with news that Queen Victoria had approved New South Wales' first constitution. Henry Parkes at once predicted that the days of 'gentry government' were numbered. The powers of colonial governors were restricted. In 1856 the first elections were held for the Legislative Assembly. They produced, in Manning Clark's ironic words, 'a government of gentlemen, rather than upstarts, levellers and red republicans' in which the pastoral, clerical and urban aristocracy won a narrow majority.

The first New South Wales premier was Stuart Donaldson, 'darling of the drawing room' and a founder of the Australian Club. He lasted less than three months before handing over to Charles Cowper. A change of government – by quiet, peaceful, democratic means. A minor miracle. Only men could vote, of course, and, depending on their property, some men could vote more than once. But it was a big advance on rule by colonial governors, or rule from London, or by a Legislative Council with members appointed for life.

The significance of that first change of government from Premier Donaldson to Premier Cowper: it was accomplished under constitutional rules, not forced by an army corps or a street mob. It had nothing to do with Eureka. It had everything to do with the expectations and ideas brought out on those eleven ships back in 1788. It was an assertion of the rule of law: the idea that not just *people* are subject to the law, but governments, too.

When these brave ideas were taking hold, most of Europe was still struggling with the idea of changing governments by democratic means. I don't want to pick on them unfairly, but we should remember that Argentina (another European settler society in the southern hemisphere with a small population in a vast land) started on more or less equal terms with us. In some ways, it had the better start: the soil was richer, markets were closer. But, as nation builders, they failed where we succeeded. Our institutions, our currency, our courts, our system of government remained robust and stable while Argentina's did not.

Why should this be so? Some of our success may be due to luck – but I don't think so. More of it was due to the strength of our institutions and the

decisions we've made about ourselves. It's about the big things Australia got right. This may be one of the reasons we're reluctant to change the Federal Constitution. In the forty-four referenda since Federation on constitutional change, only eight have succeeded. It's something that exasperates constitutional reformers like Gough Whitlam, but it reflects a determination by Australians to hold on to hard-won gains. I like that streak of obstinacy, that doggedness, that realism, that distrust of government even when it frustrates me, as with the referendum on a republic in 1999. We saw it as well when the people voted ' No' to Hughes's demand for conscription in 1916 and 1917 and Menzies' demand for banning the Communist Party in 1951.

When change really matters, Australians are ready to embrace it. But mostly we are a cautious people: prudent, vigilant, with an eye for the things that count.

Things we got right

So what are the big things we got right?

One was immigration. It wasn't something the Australian people demanded. In the post-war years, a referendum in Anglo-Celtic Australia would almost certainly have rejected large-scale immigration from southern and central Europe. But Arthur Calwell went ahead, Chifley supported him and Menzies continued the program. Even in the 1960s, a referendum in a predominantly European Australia would very probably have upheld the 'White Australia' policy. But a succession of leaders wound it back and finally ditched it.

Those decisions were right. No one now would question them. They are the best demonstration of how, in a system of strong and stable democratic government, elected leaders can lead opinion in the right direction.

This is something a robust Australian patriotism can embrace. It is impossible now to imagine a dynamic, modern Australia without its cultural and ethnic diversity. My old history book didn't say much about it. Eve Pownall was writing in 1952, and her book has a picture of a queue of disembarking immigrants, with one little girl, blonde and pigtailed, typifying the new wave. Like the German and Dutch girls from the Matraville Migrant Hostel in my 1957 class at Matraville Soldiers' Settlement Primary School. Look at Australian crowds today and try to picture a sea of all-European faces. In western countries with historically low levels of immigration – Scandinavia, say, Austria, Ireland, or Switzerland – the uniformly white faces of the crowds look odd, boring, unsettling to Australian eyes, as if somehow, at some time, life had been mysteriously frozen.

Australia, after all, might have been multicultural from the beginning. Before the Europeans arrived there were some five hundred different Aboriginal nations, each with a different language or dialect or cultural pattern. And don't forget that one persistent contention in prewar Australia was between Protestants and Catholics. A lot of energy was wasted on sectarianism. Postwar immigration introduced us to a wider world than this old sterile prejudice that alternated a police commissioner's job between the Masons and the Catholics.

Another policy we got right was the rejection of economic planning. Not even our early Labor governments wanted centralised command economies. When Menzies, in 1965, rejected the Vernon Report on the future of the economy, he rejected the kind of economic planning that had been adopted by many nations in Europe (and for which many are still paying in high unemployment and industrial ossification). On the big issues of economic reform, Australia's choices have not only been right: they have enjoyed all-party support. It was a Labor government that began the long process of deregulation in the 1980s, making possible greater competition, greater productivity and low-inflation growth.

AUSTRALIA'S GREATEST ACHIEVEMENTS

Democracy

Government selected by the people without a single military coup or instance of mob rule. Remember, liberty is not fluked – it is an achievement of a people. All our changes of government achieved democratically.

Aboriginal survival

Against the odds, despite massacre, dispossession and the onslaught of white people's diseases. The Aboriginal people's resilience is a towering achievement and a source of pride for all of us.

Australian agriculture

World competitive and increasingly smart.

A distinctive lifestyle

The creation of a way of leisure based on informality and outdoor recreation, on barbecues and bushwalks and beach picnics, thongs and shorts and lazy long weekends. 'The pursuit of happiness.'

Economic prosperity
The building of a strong and resilient national economy, with a well-paid work force protected from exploitation.

Immigration
The postwar and late-twentieth-century immigration programs, with their transformation and enrichment of Australian society. It produced the most harmonious society in the world.

The Sydney Opera House
The construction of the greatest building of the twentieth century, the pre-eminent international symbol of modern Australia.

The Sydney Olympics
The successful staging of the 2000 Olympic Games – the 'best Games ever'.

In *Thoughtlines* I mentioned other decisions we got right: winding back tariff protection, protecting large parts of the country for conservation, floating the dollar.

We were right, too, on reconciliation. The 1967 referendum giving the Commonwealth power to make laws for Aborigines (and include them in the census) was supported by more than 90 per cent of Australian voters. On this question, Australians spoke more emphatically and unambiguously than on any other public issue in our history. That historic declaration – not unmixed with love and guilt – allowed us to move forward on many things for which Aborigines had been campaigning. It led eventually to Mabo, to land rights, to ATSIC, to the awakening of Aboriginal pride in the work of their artists, in dance companies like Bangarra. It was affirmed again on 28 May 2000 when a quarter of a million of us walked across the Sydney Harbour Bridge on a bright autumn morning in support of reconciliation.

Five things to get right

More than eighty years ago, the most famous of our comic poets, C. J. Dennis, published a new national anthem, 'The Austral —— aise'. The blanks (or most of them) were meant to be filled in with what was

then known in polite circles as the 'Great Australian Adjective'.

> Fellers of Australier,
>   Blokes an' coves an' coots,
> Shift yer —— carcases,
>   Move yer —— boots.
> Gird yer —— loins up,
>   Get yer —— gun,
> Set the —— enermy
>   An' watch the —— run.

Most anthems (unlike C. J. Dennis's) proclaim a set of patriotic values. Few such values have been formally expressed in Australia's basic documents – and this, as I've said, doesn't greatly worry me. But it's as well to have a set of such values in mind. Donald Horne aimed for one when he suggested a core of Australian civic values that all of us might hold in common – what he called an 'Australian Compact', set out in a paper for the Centenary of Federation. He mentioned the rule of law, equality under the law, the need for a just and fair society – all principles I'd agree with.

But I want to suggest five other principles (or perhaps just five things to get right) as we seek a new understanding of patriotism.

First, we need a democratic consensus on population. We mustn't fall for the line that more is better. A strong, proud and confident Australia doesn't mean a bigger Australia.

Those who advocate an Australian population of fifty million aren't talking about verdant stretches of cultivated land in the central tablelands or the western plains, let alone in the continental interior. They aren't talking about inland cities, conjured into being by benevolent developers and the Burley Griffins of our time. They are talking about the urbanisation of the eastern coast from north Queensland to Melbourne: ever more housing estates, more shopping malls and multiplexes, more freeways and petrol stations where now we have rivers and forests, unpolluted beaches and open country, and in a few areas (such as Daintree or Nadgee) coastal wilderness as old as the continent itself.

James McAuley, in his satirical poem 'The True Discovery of Australia', a parody of Gulliver's report on Lilliput, gave us one sardonic commentary on our attitudes to the land:

> The place, my lord, is much like Gideon's fleece
> The second time he laid it on the ground;
> For by the will of God it has remained
> Bone-dry itself, with water all around.

Yet, as a wheel that's driven in the ruts,
It has a wet rim where the people clot
Like mud; and though they praise the inner
    spaces,
When asked to go themselves, they'd rather not.

It is still true that most new immigrants, like those before them, would spurn that bone-dry centre for the wet rim. There were visionaries in the last century who dreamt of populating the inland with peasant farmers, every family with a statutory cow and a few goats. And our early soldier settlement schemes attempted something similar – small-scale family farming. But it didn't work. Historically, most Australians opt to live near the coast, or, at any rate, east of the Great Divide. There is nothing sentimental in a policy that seeks to preserve as much of the beauty of our coast as possible. The course I advocate is in fact a rather tough, pragmatic and self-interested one: it's about preserving economic competitiveness in world markets. Let's keep Australia affluent *and* beautiful, especially in those parts of it where most of us want to live.

The second thing I'd like to see is a patriotism based on education. An ignorant patriot would be the worst kind of all. It's why we have introduced classes in civics and government in schools in New South Wales. It's why I've done everything I can to

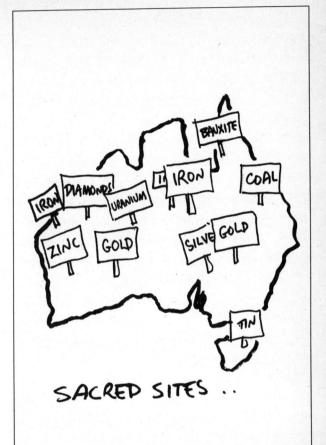

SACRED SITES ..

encourage the teaching of history. It is why we have refocused education in New South Wales on the basics, especially literacy – with great results, thanks to the teachers. We've all heard appalling stories of the ignorance of American children: unable to name their first president or the dates of the Civil War. The best safeguard for democracy is an educated electorate. No one can respect a country that forces its universities to abandon courses and staff positions. If Australia is to be internationally competitive we don't need a population of fifty million with unequal standards of education. I'd rather have twenty million people with the best education in the world.

That means – it's my third idea – a renewed respect for the public sector. Whenever I hear people criticise public servants as slackers or fat cats, I ask which public servants they mean: teachers, lecturers, doctors, nurses, police, firefighters, the armed services, bus and train drivers, museum curators, librarians, judges, scientists, economists, civil engineers, town planners? Teachers and nurses need people to speak up for them. I read a wonderful comment from Dr John Buchanan, deputy director of the University of Sydney's Centre for Industrial Relations Research and Training. In recent years, he said, 'we sent out a signal that the greatest heroes were the fund managers, merchant bankers and business consultants. In the process we relegated those who educate our society, maintain the laws and tend the sick to the status of losers.' I look forward to a time when our front-line public servants will be no less esteemed than the go-getters and tax dodgers, the overpaid and underachieving executives, the self-styled high-flyers and jumped-up celebrities who dominate the gossip columns.

My fourth suggestion is this: let's be more demanding when it comes to citizenship rights. Patriotism thrives on a sense of inclusiveness, of belonging, a collective sense of being special. Citizenship needs to be more highly valued. I think it's fair to expect, in candidates for naturalisation, some understanding of our civil and political institutions. I agree with Horne when he says that immigrants should be encouraged to take up the idea of an Australian Compact – those core civic values we can all share.

Finally, a healthy patriotism needs opportunities to proclaim itself. We still argue about the design of the flag. Well-meaning people keep coming up with new ones. One day, if Australians wish, the flag may change. But the best reason for keeping the one we have is that it says something about our history and geography. It depicts, in the Federal star, something of our political structure. As a couple in a Central Coast retirement village said, 'Don't change the flag,

Bob, or not until *we've* passed on.' The change will come if and when people see it as natural – and then it will happen without a fuss.

And let's have no more nagging disputes about whether 26 January is the best date for our national commemoration. Of course it is. Aborigines won't all agree, but they can have a special perspective on their celebration too. Already they claim 26 January as Survival Day, and what they remember on that day is part of what other Australians remember. So let's celebrate – and mourn – together. We should honour our achievements together as we remember our sufferings together. It's part of our genius as a nation that we can trace our institutions back to that summer's day in January, two hundred and fifteen years ago, when a collection of sore and weary voyagers clambered ashore from their long-boats.

I know some may not share this vision for Australia, but I hope we'll keep working for the republic. It surprises me how many people say, 'I believe we'll have a republic one day; it's inevitable', yet don't want to think about it now. Here's a first step, a simple way to achieve much of what re-publicans were aiming for in 1999: declare the Governor-General our head of state. Few would oppose it. Instead of talking about a 'republic', talk about the 'Commonwealth' – that wonderfully generous and expressive term used by republicans in the seventeenth century and adopted as the label for our own democracy in 1901.

The *Commonwealth* of Australia! Let's keep that special word for our country. Let's be proud of it. And if 'Governor-General' sounds strange for a head of state, so what? A titular head of state (as opposed to an executive president – which few want) is a strange job, anyway. It warrants an exotic name. Remember: we're a funny country.

Reconciling past and present

As a boy I lived around the beaches and sand dunes of Sydney's southern suburbs. In May 1770, soon after his first landing at Kurnell, Cook came ashore at Botany Bay and made his way with a party of men along the coast past Little Bay and Malabar to Maroubra, not far from where I live now. It was the year Beethoven was born.

'Nothing remarkable,' wrote Cook in his journal, 'barren heath diversified with marshes and morasses.' This was Aboriginal land; its indigenous owners were among the first to succumb to the white man's smallpox.

Always the most difficult thing about a contemporary Australian patriotism will be reconciling our pride in modern Australia, our love of its freedoms

MY SACRED SITES

The sandstone cliffs and coastal heath that sweep south from Botany Bay along what is now the **Royal National Park** (declared in 1879, the second-oldest national park in the world). From these ledges indigenous people saw the ghost-white sails of the *Endeavour* and, eighteen years later, Phillip's ominous First Fleet and, days later, La Perouse's doomed vessels hovering in the sea-mist. Botany Bay saw these fantastically garbed interlopers from London, Paris, Irish farms and the rotting prison hulks of the Thames. Extraordinary encounters took place, as in interplanetary travel, between unknowing, baffled strangers from different universes upon these rocks, amid this vegetation.

Byron Bay, perhaps the most eccentric paradise Australia affords tall rainforests, jagged mountains, unending creamy beaches. What was once a whaling town is now (since the passage of marine mammals protection laws introduced in 1986 by the then Environment Minister Bob Carr) a place where dolphins surf unthreatened, watched by crowds from the world's best-positioned lighthouse.

The Kowmung Valley, Blue Mountains. A river runs between steep, forested cliffs. Sandbanks, islands, occasional big, deep, sky-blue mountain pools restore to your sight the ancient wild continent that was Terra Australis, a mystery and a wonder to all who ventured near it.

Sydney Harbour, part of it still as it was in 1788, part of it visibly present in the paintings of the eighteenth and nineteenth centuries, but most of it the metropolitan wonder we see today: waterside restaurants, skyscrapers, islands with convict buildings, the bridge and Opera House in an unrolling mural unequalled anywhere. Here troops sailed for Gallipoli and came home, on crutches and stretchers, from the Somme, Kokoda and Long Tan. Here the Tall Ships returned in 1988; here, every New Year, we celebrate with fireworks.

In Canberra, the **Australian War Memorial**. I write about it on pages 31 to 33, but it stands for me as a reminder of the most significant fact in Australia's twentieth-century history: the loss of 61 720 Australian lives in World War I.

In Canberra, too, **Old Parliament House**: in its municipal Art Deco rooms, corridors and chambers were played out the politics of the Depression, World War II, the Cold War, the transition to Whitlam and the crisis of 1975, the advent of Hawke. (It's nearby in new Parliament House that I found the marvellous quote from Marcus Clarke that appears on page ix.) The old place stands for something: it stands for the people of Australia electing their own representatives and governing themselves. That is, it stands for our democracy.

and institutions, its special beauty, with our knowledge of what was done to the indigenous people.
How is it possible to be proud of a heritage that
brought suffering, death and disease to so many?

In many respects Australia is better than it was. We
no longer cling to 'White Australia' – the doctrine of
white supremacy that seemed axiomatic for more
than a hundred years. We no longer relegate women to
second-rate status. We've left behind the sectarianism
that disfigured social and public life, setting Catholic
against Protestant in the pre-war years. We've out-
grown the pernicious wowserism that ruled our
cities for so long, that stifling crusade against pleasure
in any form. We no longer practise the most repressive
censorship in the western world. We no longer
persecute homosexuals. We no longer permit the
destruction of our heritage buildings, so many torn
down by developers in the frenzied booms of the
1960s and 1970s. We are beginning to preserve and
restore the natural environment – so much of what
fell to the axe, the chainsaw, the harpoon, the gun, the
poisoned stream.

The mistakes of the past were not uniquely ours.
All countries can point to similar misfortunes; ours
are akin to those of other European settler societies in
the so-called New World. But if Australia Day is to be
an occasion for celebrating what we are and what we

have been, then the best and worst of our story needs to be acknowledged.

There can be no point in trying to invent resentments against Britain or denying the value of her gifts. The great thing we owe to our British origins is that authority in Australia has passed without bloodshed from one administration to the next for more than a century and a half. Tocqueville, that great French observer of the American story, was wrong when he said that 'of all the British colonies, Australia is the only one deprived of those precious liberties which constitute the glory of England and the strengths of its offshoots in all parts of the world'. Nowhere in the world are those liberties more secure. John Douglas Pringle, an admiring chronicler of Australian ways, put it well nearly fifty years ago, in *Australian Accent*:

> When all is said, everything that Britain could do for Australia as a nation was done long ago. Britain discovered Australia [for the Europeans], founded her as a place to dump her criminals, governed her, peopled her, nourished her and finally set her free. Australia long ago repaid any debt there was a hundred times over with the blood of her young men killed in three wars. There is nothing to regret; the slate is rubbed

clean. Australia's future is as an independent nation.

Try this test in Sydney. Go to Dawes Point Reserve, that little piece of ground in The Rocks, where all the city's main landmarks can be seen. Go there at night. From here you can see the Harbour Bridge, a luminescent Opera House, a spangled skyline, quiet gardens, Luna Park with all its febrile ornamentation, old ship moorings, a busy expressway, tourist vessels and sailing boats not far from where Phillip anchored, modern ferries, taxis, crowds, immigrant faces pressed to mobile phones. From nowhere else can all this be seen together. Or walk through some of our coastal bushland on a summer's day, glimpse the surf through a fringe of eucalyptus and see ordinary Australian families at leisure. Not long ago on Hyams Beach at Jervis Bay I passed an Aboriginal family, then an Indian one, then a Chinese–Australian group; and there was Helena with me, with her mixed Chinese–Indian heritage.

So think of Australians as I do: a resilient, pragmatic, good-humoured people, generous and humane, aware of their fantastic natural inheritance. The patriotism I'm sketching would draw on all this. It would celebrate a mature people, comfortable with our origins, at peace with our neighbours, reconciled at last with the people whose country we stole.

Would Phillip, if he were to stand at Dawes Point today, not be proud of what he saw? Should indigenous Australians not be proud as well? The Aboriginal people, by their defiant survival, have asserted their rights. Reconciliation – that great movement of healing, begun in the aftermath of suffering and shame – must go forward, taking different forms and shapes. Until we can all feel that it has been accomplished, in a great national act of contrition and goodwill, our celebration of Australia Day will never be entirely complete.

What we celebrate in this funny, friendly, happy country is a story of survival and achievement. Our conversation with our history should give us confidence in our future. We may well bear another terrorist attack. But we know how Australians have withstood losses – the immense casualities of two world wars. We can take comfort from that. We may have big economic choices to make as well: a trade pact with the United States, closer economic ties with China. And this shouldn't daunt us either. We've taken big decisions before. We got most of the economic policies right in recent years – it's why our living standards grew strongly in the 1990s.

Eve Pownall knew none of this, of course. But she knew our toughness, our ingenuity. She understood the courage and resourcefulness of the Australian people. Speaking to her young readers on the last page of my history book, she asked us to be grateful, to look ahead with confidence, to rejoice in the beauty of the land – 'its timberlands and beaches, its vineyards and its gold' – and to remember the sailors, the explorers, the pioneers, the first owners. 'They wrote,' as she put it, 'the first pages of Australia's story, and today the story goes on. Like you, it is living and growing.'

The author's proceeds from this book will go to assist Bali victims, survivors and their families.

Acknowledgements

The quotation on page 18 from Eric Rolls's essay 'The Nature of Australia', in Tom Griffiths and Libby Robin: *Ecology and Empire* (1997), is reproduced by kind permission of Melbourne University Press.

The extract on pages 71 and 72 from *Australian Accent* by John Douglas Pringle, published by Chatto & Windus (1957), is used by kind permission of The Random House Group Limited.

Every effort has been made to contact the copyright holders of material reproduced in this book and the publishers would welcome any further information.